LEAP

First Edition: 2019
ISBN: 9781686213052

Alexandria S. Norton
PO BOX 703
Griffith, IN 46319

Although the author and publisher have made every effort to ensure that the information in this book was correct at press time, the author and publisher do not assume and hereby disclaim, any liability to any party for any loss, damage, or disruption caused by errors or omissions, whether such errors or omissions result from negligence, accident, or any other cause.

Cover Design by Adarah
Edited by Denise Sarkor at New Roots Press
Book formatting by Nelly Murariu at PixBeeDesign.com

LEAP

ALEXANDRIA S. NORTON

Foreword by Andria S. Hudson

This book is dedicated to the
next generation of leaders and trailblazers.

May you walk boldly in your kingly authority.
May you be fearless and uncompromising in your pursuit of
your kingdom assignment. **YOU ARE UNSTOPPABLE.**

In JESUS' name. Amen.

CONTENTS

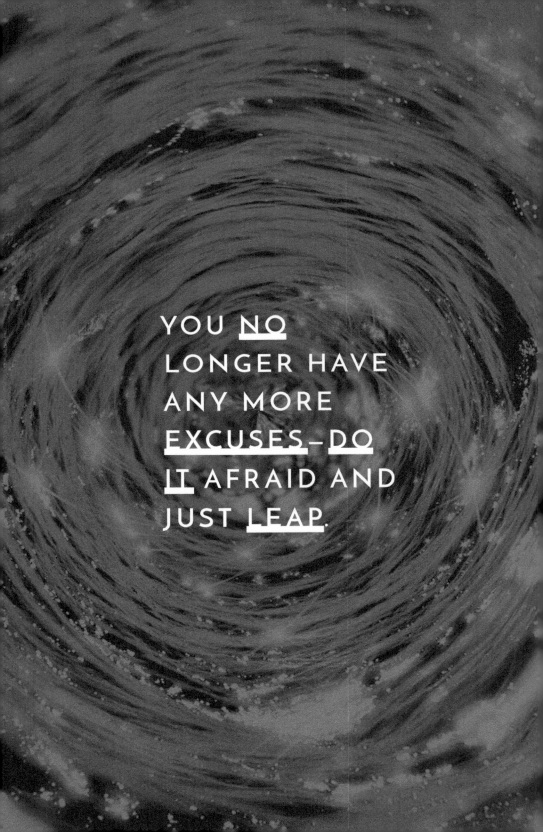

YOU <u>NO</u> LONGER HAVE ANY MORE <u>EXCUSES</u>—<u>DO IT</u> AFRAID AND JUST <u>LEAP</u>.

FOREWORD

Living life to its fullest dimensions requires an individual to have the following: faith, focus, and freedom. The concept of faith is very simple although we have made it quite complicated. Faith is the complete confidence and trust in something and someone without physical proof. We utilize faith for the simplest tasks in our daily lives without really thinking about it. We drive on man-made streets, fly in airplanes, and dine at various eateries and restaurants without question or hesitation. However, when it comes to us taking measures of faith to live above mediocrity, the average or mundane, that's when the fight begins. The fight begins when your faith begins. When you choose to walk in faith and live by faith, fear—perverted faith—will attempt to hold you hostage, capture your focus, and contain you from living the life of freedom and peace that God designed for you to have.

In this book by author Alexandria Norton, the concepts of faith and freedom are beautifully expressed. She addresses the issues of fear, self-doubt, uncertainty and how to conquer them all. She also gives the reader a look into her own personal challenges and how she rose above them. The vernacular of this book will assure you that you are not alone. The best way to accomplish a goal or a dream is to do it afraid. The longer you reason, analyze, and question what God has called you to do something, the more complacent you become. Alexandria offers biblical scriptures, practical wisdom, and transparency to motivate you to just LEAP. As you read this book, you will begin to see your life through the LOVELY eyes of God—His will, His desire, and His purpose for your life. This book will challenge you to take the necessary steps of faith to live out your best life in God.

You no longer have any more excuses—do it afraid and just LEAP. There's a new world of freedom waiting on you.

Selah.

Andria S. Hudson

INTRODUCTION

It was all a LEAP.

LEAP: *To make a large jump or sudden movement, usually from one place to another.*

(Cambridge Dictionary)

The most defining moments of my life started with a LEAP. As a matter of fact, this whole book was a LEAP. It was a LARGE jump, a sudden movement to act on the word of God. Although I am not sure where or how far this book will go or whose hands it will fall into, there is one thing that is certain. I LEAPED! Afraid and certain, I LEAPED. Never written or published a book. LEAPED. Feeling disqualified and inadequate. LEAPED, LEAPED!

God is going to call you to make decisions and make major moves that require a LEAP—a leap to start a business, a leap to move from your hometown, a leap to get a degree, a leap to marry, a leap to leave that no-good boyfriend (or girlfriend) of yours, a leap to start an organization, a leap to sow into someone. Whatever God tells you do, just LEAP. Do it afraid, do it without having all the pieces to the puzzle, do it 'broke' because you're not broke anyway. Your heavenly Father happens to own cattle on a thousand hills (*Psalm 50:10*). It does not matter how young or old you are. LEAP.

This book was crafted to serve as a manual for each and every person who will trust God with their whole life and just LEAP. It is

DO IT AFRAID,
DO IT WITHOUT
HAVING ALL THE
PIECES TO
THE PUZZLE.

jam-packed with biblical references, personal experiences, and quotes to enlighten, encourage, and empower you to LEAP into your destiny.

My prayer for you is that you will find the heart and the mind of the Father in this book. I pray that His thoughts and desires concerning your move(s), will be revealed to you. I pray that you will hear God like never before and take heed to His instructions. I pray that everything that has been holding you back, will abruptly fall as you LEAP. I pray that as you LEAP, blessings and miracles will come to you by LEAPS AND BOUNDS. More importantly, I pray that if you do not know Jesus, this book will lead you to salvation. He is the truth, the way, and the life (John 14:6). I cannot LIVE, nor LEAP, without Him and I pray you will find this to be true personally.

LET'S LEAP!

PART I

WHATEVER _GOD_ HAS CALLED YOU TO DO, HE HAS ALREADY _EQUIPPED YOU_ FOR IT AND HE HAS ALREADY PROVIDED ALL OF THE NECESSARY _RESOURCES_.

"I ain't never scared."

—BONE CRUSHER

Our reluctance or resistance to taking leaps is often driven by fear—fear of the unknown, fear of change, fear of failure, and the list goes on. But what I have learned is that, when we set our minds or our focus to do something great, we can expect fear to present itself. We can expect fear to show up and give us every reason why our efforts will not work. We can expect fear to pop up, often manifesting as every excuse in the book.

According to the Merriam Webster dictionary, fear is defined as "an unpleasant, often strong emotion caused by anticipation or awareness of danger."

Before I started IAMBELOVED, I remember how afraid I was. In the beginning stages, IAMBELOVED was just a blog. I had no intention or vision of it becoming what it is today. However, even as a blog, I was met with fear—fear that it wouldn't be as successful as I desired it to be. I feared that no one would read it. I feared that it would be just another blog and I would become an ordinary blogger among all the other emerging bloggers at that time. However, I realized that IAMBELOVED was something God had placed on my heart. God had given me a passion and desire to help broken and lost young women. God had initiated this urgency within me to help restore confidence into young women. God had given me this baby to carry and birth. So, if God gave it to me, it wasn't my job to make it successful—it was His. My job was to be obedient and allow him to lead me. My job was to LEAP, and so I did. In just two years, this 'ordinary blog' has helped thousands of young women. IAMBELOVED has been able to give back to the community. IAMBELOVED is now a thriving foundation that continues to encourage, empower, and equip young women today, all because I refused to allow fear to hold me hostage.

I love God so much because He never breaks a promise. In the scripture Isaiah 41:10, God admonishes His people to not be afraid and He makes a promise to help them and give them strength. This lets me know that the assignment God has given me comes with His assistance. No matter what God calls you to do, you can EXPECT that He will make sure that you have what you need.

I love the story of Joshua (if you've never read it, I strongly encourage you to do so!). In the first chapter of the book of Joshua, we find God giving Joshua a command, or assignment. It's a pretty big assignment, one that I would have definitely asked God if He was sure He wanted me to do it. But I love how God tells Joshua to be strong and of courage in the midst of giving him the assignment. He literally tells Joshua this three times. I questioned God as to why, and He reminded me of how the children of Israel were initially afraid to go over to the promise land. They had every excuse for why they should not go, but these views were promoted by fear (*Numbers 13*). So, in order for Joshua to complete the assignment, he had to be strong and courageous. If Joshua allowed the fears of the people to encompass him, he would not have been able to go to the promise land. God encouraged Joshua, shielding him from the fear that presented itself to the children of Israel.

Likewise, God wants you to be strong and courageous too. The children of God do not need to fear ANYTHING because God is always with us (*Deuteronomy 31:6*). You can rest, knowing that whatever God has called you to do, He has already equipped you for it and He has already provided all of the necessary resources. Refuse to allow the enemy to torment you with fear. If he can get you to become afraid, he can get you to quit. Remember the enemy comes to steal, kill, and destroy (*John 10:10*). I truly believe one of his favorite tactics or strategies is to impose fear on the people of God. If he can steal your faith or confidence, he can prevent you from moving into all that God has for you. But remember Beloved, God did not give us the spirit of fear, but of power, of love, and a sound mind (*2 Timothy 1:7*).

AFFIRMATION

I am bold, I am courageous, and I am fearless because God is with me.

SCRIPTURES

1. Isaiah 41:10

2. Deuteronomy 31:6

3. 2 Timothy 1:7

REFLECTION

I will overcome my fears by _____

_____

_____

IF <u>GOD</u> HAS
CHOSEN OR
HANDPICKED YOU
FOR AN <u>ASSIGNMENT</u>,
KNOW THAT HE DID NOT
MAKE A MISTAKE.

CHAPTER 2

Enough is...ENOUGH.

O ne of the biggest issues I have personally encountered and known others to struggle with, is the deep-seated feeling of inadequacy. I have literally lost track of how many times I have either felt, or told myself, that I was not enough—not enough for the job, not enough to start the blog, not enough for marriage, etc. I simply felt that I wasn't good enough for anything. When we allow thoughts or feelings of inadequacy or inferiority to control our minds, we never move forward. We will never leap if we succumb to these types of thoughts.

Sometimes you do feel like you are enough, but you also feel like you do not *have* enough. Sometimes the greatest challenge we face before we leap, is a perceived insufficiency of resources. Not enough money, not enough space, or not enough help, are some common concerns. As human beings if we cannot see everything at once, then we do not pursue it. Now, I do strongly believe in strategic planning; I do believe in proper preparation. However, if we always waited around until we had 'enough,' we would never move forward, we would never leap. What I've also come to realize is that God does not always show us the whole puzzle. He just gives us a piece at a time and that can be so frustrating because we often have no clue of how something will turn out. I struggle with this so badly sometimes!

I am not the type of person who can just sit and ride. I have to know where we are going, why we are we going there, and who's all going to be there. Lol! I have to know! So, when God takes me through the seasons where it's just 'piece by piece,' I tend to get frustrated or worse, I want to give up. But it's in these moments, or seasons, where I learn to trust God the most. Even when the circumstances don't make sense, God always knows what He is doing.

When I think about all of this, I am reminded of the story in Luke where Jesus tells Simon to "put out into deep water and let down the nets for a catch." (*Luke 5:4 NIV*) He gives Simon an assignment, a task. Simon responds, "Master, we've worked hard all night and haven't caught anything." (verse 5) When I think about this statement from Simon Peter, I begin to wonder why that was the first thing he said. Then the Lord revealed to me the times when He has given me instructions and I responded out of exhaustion, frustration, uncertainty, fear, or inadequacy. I have questioned God multiple times if He was sure about a matter. I have asked God if He was sure it was me He wanted to use. I have questioned if He was sure it was the right move for me to make. I've questioned God or made certain statements because the present circumstances did not *appear* to line up with His instructions. Similarly, Simon was tired. He and the other fishermen had already been dropping nets and expecting fish, but received nothing thus far. And can we blame him? In this moment, I would have felt as if something wasn't *enough*. The nets weren't enough, maybe my skills as a fisherman weren't *enough*. But in the second clause of that scripture, we read Simon's response: "But because You say so, I will let down the nets." WOW!

Regardless of how he felt at that moment, because JESUS told him to do it, whatever tiredness, doubts, or discouragement he felt, could not outweigh Jesus. He TRUSTED Jesus. How many of us can say that we trust Jesus more than our fears or feelings?

We can learn from Simon. We can learn that the way to overcome the feelings or beliefs that we are not enough, is by choosing to put our faith and trust in God. We can choose to take God at His word. We can choose to believe that God is God and He knows exactly what He is doing, even if we don't yet comprehend what's happening.

So, if God has chosen or handpicked you for an assignment, know that He did not make a mistake. He did not look at a list and accidently pick you. He knows exactly what He's doing. Wherever you are lacking, God will fill that area. It is God that makes up the difference. It is His GRACE that enables you to complete the assignment. His GRACE provides everything you need to get the job done.

If you were able to do everything yourself, if you were capable in your own skills or talents or abilities, then where would you give God glory? You are enough for God to use, but not enough without Him. It is He that works in us and through us (*Acts 17:28*).

Last thing, when Simon trusted Jesus and launched his net, the Bible tells us that "*they caught a great number of fish, and their nets were [at the point of] breaking*" (AMP version) They had more than enough! Amazing, right?!

Trust God, not those negative feelings or thoughts that control you. You are enough because God specifically handpicked you!

AFFIRMATION

I am enough
and I have enough
because of
God's grace.

SCRIPTURES

1. Luke 5:4-6

2. 2 Corinthians 12:9

3. Philippians 4:13

REFLECTION

I will remember that I am enough by _____

_____

_____

CHAPTER 3

"How many times do I have to tell you?"

A FRUSTRATED PARENT

I cannot begin to tell you how many times in my life I have responded to something with the words: "I don't know about this." Lol! When it came time for me to be promoted at my job, I literally told my boss, "I don't know about this." Now, I had the audacity to say this after the Lord had spoken to me months before, telling me that I would be promoted. This was actually after I APPLIED for the promotion and received word that I did not need to apply because I was being considered. This was after I had consciously waited and waited to be promoted. What nerve I had responding with "I don't know about this!" I'm pretty sure God was sitting on His throne like, "Girl, WHAT!" I'm pretty sure God put His hand over His head, shaking it like, "how many times do I have to tell this child."

I remember when my fiancé and I were dating and whenever he would tell me something my response would be, "are you sure?" It would annoy him greatly. Lol. I didn't realize, until now, just how much I doubted in the past. I was often uncertain about a lot of things then. I was uncertain about launching IAMBELOVED. Actually, I was uncertain before taking action on any great thing that I wanted to pursue. I doubted God's plan and vision often. But these experiences taught me that where there is a great assignment, doubt or uncertainty will emerge.

These experiences reminded me of the story of the two spies—Joshua and Caleb. The story that starts when they and other spies were sent out by Moses to the land of Canaan. Canaan was the land that God had PROMISED to give to the children of Israel (*Numbers 13:2*). The spies went, checked out the land, and brought back a report. The report was that the land was indeed good and everything God had promised—the land surely flowed with milk and honey (*Numbers 13:27*). The spies went as far as showing fruit from the land. Joshua and Caleb told the children of Israel EVERYTHING they saw, including the type of people:

> *"But the people who live there are powerful, and the cities are fortified and very large. We even saw descendants of Anak there. 29 The Amalekites live in the Negev; the Hittites, Jebusites and Amorites live in the hill country; and the Canaanites live near the sea and along the Jordan."*

I interpreted this to mean 'we even saw the Doubters there.' The Naysayers, the Haters, and the Backbiters, all live in the hill. And the Gossipers, they live there too!

But here's the part I laughed at. With all that information, Caleb responded, "let's go up at once, and possess it, for we are well able to overcome it." (verse 30) You mean to tell me that all these crazy people are in this land that the Lord promised? I am certain that my response would have been "you sure?" or "I don't know about this."

THERE ARE OPPORTUNITIES WE MISS WHEN WE DOUBT.

I am very sure that in that moment, doubt would have risen up in me, and that is actually what happened with the children of Israel. They were fearful and DOUBTFUL. They took their focus off of the promise of God and placed it on the report. Isn't that what we do at times? God has made so many promises to each of us, but one negative thing or one negative thought can cause us to be uncertain. One bad experience can cause us to question God and God is asking us, "what did I just tell you?"

If you read further in the text, you see that because Caleb trusted God, God promised that Caleb would be allowed to enter the land (*Numbers 14:24*). Then, you read God's response for those who doubted:

> "*Doubtless ye shall not come into the land, concerning which I sware to make you dwell therein, save Caleb the son of Jephunneh, and Joshua the son of Nun.*"

There is a price we pay when we give into doubt. There are opportunities we miss when we doubt.

Every assignment or task God gives you will not always be easy. Some things REQUIRE your absolute faith and trust in His word. There will be challenges and obstacles, but you have to decide that you will believe every word that God says.

If God told you to write the book, find a pen and start writing. If God told you to start the business, get your plan together. If God told you to move, pack your bags! Don't delay your promise by doubting.

God has a plan for you (*Jeremiah 29:11*) and it's not to harm you or hurt you, but you must trust and not doubt.

AFFIRMATION

I am well able to
do it because God
made me a promise.

SCRIPTURES

1. Numbers 13:30
2. Mark 11:23
3. Jeremiah 17:7-8
4. Proverbs 29:25
5. Hebrews 6:12

REFLECTION

Write down 5 promises to remember when you face any doubt.

God promised me _____, _____,

_____, _____,

_____.

CHAPTER 4

Get past your past.

There have been so many times where I felt that I was undeserving of anything great because of my past. The mistakes I made and the failures I encountered all led me to believe that I was completely unworthy of doing anything God called me to do. Past hurts and disappointments, and past heartbreaks almost paralyzed me. I remember a time where my heart was completely broken. I mean BROKEN, shattered. I experienced a breakup that felt like someone had just abruptly and unexpectedly died. Months had passed and I began feeling depressed, a depression that caused me to almost lose my complete focus.

I was so busy looking back that looking forward became a real challenge. I looked back multiple times, wishing I did things differently. I looked back for an apology. I looked back wondering how something that once was, could just completely fall apart. I was distracted by my past.

Your story may be different from mine, but many of us have experienced being so focused on the past that the future began to look nonexistent. Each time you tried to move forward, something from the past pulled you back. For example, every time I made a few steps forward, my mind would replay a moment where someone told me I wasn't good enough or that I didn't deserve to have them in my life. My mind would begin to repeat all of the negative words spoken to me. My mind would recall the times I failed and then, before I knew it, I was in a sunken place.

YOUR PAST CAN NEVER OVERRULE YOUR FUTURE WHEN YOU DECIDE TO KEEP MOVING FORWARD.

So how did I overcome? I prayed, I read scriptures and I rehearsed them. I meditated on scripture daily. As terrible as my singing is, I sang until I felt better. I talked to trusted people, who encouraged me. I got up when I did not feel like it, I showered, I put on makeup, and I ate. The point I am trying to make is that I KEPT MOVING FORWARD. I took it one day at a time. I wrote encouraging messages and scriptures on post-its and placed them on my mirror and my wall at work. When I felt down or discouraged, I read these messages to myself until I believed them for myself. I pressed through it, I cried through it, I dragged my feet through it. I took a break if I needed to, and I got right back to living my life.

In seasons where I felt that my past was clouding my mind, I would lean on the scripture Philippians 3:13 (amplified version) where Paul states, "Brothers and sisters, I do not consider that I have made it my own yet; but one thing I *do*: forgetting what *lies* behind and reaching forward to what *lies* ahead."

Notice what he said! He FORGETS everything behind him and reaches forward toward what lies AHEAD! Get this, the past will try to call and pull you backwards, but you have to REACH forward! Past habits, past thoughts, past friends, past baes, past mindsets, REACH! REACH for what lies ahead and then, LEAP!

Your past can never overrule your future when you decide to keep moving forward. So, go forward. GO FORTH! Destiny is ahead of you, not behind you.

AFFIRMATION

My past cannot
and will not hold
me back!

SCRIPTURES

1. Isaiah 26:3

2. Isaiah 43:18-19

3. 2 Corinthians 10:5

4. Philippians 3:13

REFLECTION

I will overcome my past by _____

_____

_____

_____

CHAPTER 5

It's in the house!

If I could count all the times I was reluctant to do something—or leap, I wouldn't have enough fingers and toes left to count! Seriously. Every time I felt a nudge or push from God to make a move, one of my biggest reasons for not moving forward would be because I **felt,** or it **appeared** as if, I did not have enough. The vision was always greater than the provision. The idea was always greater than the resources I had. But I remember one day, when I was struggling with an idea, an old good friend of mine said, "if **God** gave the **vision,** **He** will make **provision**." I will never forget that moment because it helped me realize that if this was God's idea, then God will provide everything I need, all I had to do was say 'yes.' All I had to do was take the reliance off of myself and place my trust in God. After planning multiple successful events, my team and I developed a motto which goes, "God will do what we cannot do, all we have to do is what we are able to do." This motto helps us keep in mind that God entrusted us with this vision and we are to carry out and deliver this vision with excellence in partnership with the Holy Spirit.

The vision that God has placed inside of you, already has resources lined up. God is just waiting for you to make the first step. God is just waiting on you to LEAP.

WHENEVER WE FEEL AS IF WE DO NOT HAVE SOMETHING, GOD IS SAYING TO DO A THOROUGH INVENTORY CHECK!

Many times, we complain about a lack of resources when the resources are right in our hands. We complain and often, the resources are right in OUR HOUSE! In other words, what do you ALREADY have?

I am reminded of the story of Elisha and the widow when I think of situations where it seems as if the resources are absent. In 2 Kings 4:1-7 the story tells of a widow that went to Elisha with a sense of entitlement. In hopes to receive help to pay off a debt, the widow informs Elisha that her husband—one of Elisha's servants—was dead. Elisha then asked the woman, "what do you have in your house?" The widow responded, "your servant has nothing there at all, except a small jar of olive oil."

PAUSE! How many times have you thought you lacked something, but once you reflected a bit more, you remembered that the thing did exist? It may not be the very thing you need exactly, but you have SOMETHING.

For example, I've had many moments where I've been so broke that I lacked the funds to buy food. I would say that I have nothing to eat, but then realize, I had a bag of Idaho potatoes in the fridge. NOW, I may not have had the ingredients for a whole meal, but if I used my creativity, I could make some fries! Get it?

Whenever we feel as if we do not have something, God is saying to do a thorough inventory check! It is in those moments when we do not have what we need, that we CREATE what we need!

Now, back to the story. Elisha then told the widow to "go around and ask all your neighbors for empty jars. Don't ask for just a few. Then go inside and shut the door behind you and your sons. Pour oil into all the jars, and as each is filled, put it to one side." Not only does God have resources, He has people lined up to give you what you need! As the widow filled the jars, each jar was filled with oil! The little oil she started off with became what she needed to pay off her debts.

I want you to know that although the resources seem nonexistent, God will provide! Even if you don't know where the money will come from to fund the vision—to start the business, to write the book, to purchase the home, to coordinate the event, GOD WILL PROVIDE.

One last thing, I love how Elisha told the woman, "go, sell the oil and pay your debts. You and your sons can live on **what is left.**"

So not only will God provide everything you need, but it'll also be more than enough. You will have excess.

LEAP woman! LEAP man! God's got you!

AFFIRMATION

God has already made provision for the vision. I shall have everything that I need and more.

SCRIPTURES

1.   2 Kings 4:1-7

2.   Matthew 6:31-34

3.   2 Corinthians 9:8

4.   Philippians 4:19

REFLECTION

I trust God to provide for _____

_____

_____

CHAPTER 6

"What are you waiting for?"

NICKELBACK

Now, I do not particularly struggle in this area anymore, but procrastination and laziness are serious issues. I have seen the detrimental effects of laziness and procrastination from those around me. Some of them do not realize it and then some have actually admitted that they have a procrastination issue. I have heard people share with me their goals and visions for their lives, while the refrain from taking the proper steps towards their goals. They are STUCK, and they are stuck for more than one reason. Procrastination is not uncommon; however, you must first figure out why you procrastinate? Do you function better under pressure? Is there an urgency to get "it" done? Are you distracted? What is causing the delay? It is vitally important that you identify the reason why you do it. This way, once you identify the cause or reason, you will be able to overcome it.

This chapter is to serve you notice that it is time to get up and get moving. Just START. Start with what you have and what you know, and make the first step. You may not have it all figured out just yet, but if there is a goal, if there is an idea, if there is a dream, it is in your power to make the first step.

LEAP

The great thing about a leap is that it doesn't require that both feet land at the same time. A leap starts with one foot moving forward and then, the other foot follows shortly behind. So, take that one step. Make that one small change. Go to sleep early so you can rise in the morning to do what needs to be done. Put your phone on *do not disturb* so you can focus. Withdraw from the relationships or friendships that are holding you back. Break unsupportive habits.

I knew two years ago that I was going to write a book. The Lord told me. However, it took me about two years to even START writing this book. I procrastinated. I had never written a book before. I did not know where to even start and so, I pushed it off. The Lord told me again, two more times, that it was time to write the book, yet I still procrastinated. I felt that I did not have the time to focus on writing a book. But then, once I realized that writing this book was bigger than me, it became urgent to start. Once I realized that this book wasn't just for me, but also for you and the other millions of lives that will read it, I started. I started with a title. Next, an objective arose; I found my WHY. I created a deadline, which I had to extend (side note: it's ok if it takes longer than expected, just keep going). Then, I leaped. It started with one chapter a day, some days produced two chapters and finally, the book was finished, published and now, you are reading it.

If you are stuck, I challenge you today to find your WHY. Begin to see the faces of people whose lives will be changed by what God has placed inside of you.

The Bible tells us in Ephesians 2:10 that we were created in Christ Jesus to do good WORKS, which God prepared in advance for us to do. God created you to do a good work.

Get up, get moving, and LEAP!

BEGIN TO SEE THE
FACES OF PEOPLE
WHOSE LIVES
WILL BE CHANGED
BY WHAT GOD
HAS PLACED
INSIDE OF YOU.

AFFIRMATION

There are people who need what God has placed inside of me. It's bigger than me.

SCRIPTURES

1. Proverbs 18:9

2. Proverbs 24: 33-34

3. Ephesians 2:10

REFLECTION

I will overcome my procrastination by _____

_____

_____

PART II

CHAPTER 7

Remember your WHY.

Sometimes the reason we are unable to take a leap, is because we have not identified our WHY. We have not identified why this leap is necessary and we have not identified who the leap is for. It is rather easy to become consumed with ourselves, but I wrote this chapter to inform and remind you that the leap is much bigger than you. It is NOT all about you.

There are people whose lives are waiting on a change to come and that change is connected to your leap. Think about the people or the things that have helped and changed your life. I think about Marlena Banks and The Big Idea Food book. Although I knew I would write this book, after reading a few chapters of Big Idea Food, my whole perspective changed and that simple act gave me the courage I needed to start writing my own book. Marlena's book was written for aspiring authors like me. Think about Apple and the iPhone (sorry androids); think about how this innovative company has created many products that have helped and continue to help millions of people. I think about the many times I attended church and was blessed because my Pastor preached a word that was designed just for me and everyone else in the congregation. If my Pastor decided to stay quiet and reject his calling, I wonder where I would be at this moment! If Jesus got off the cross, where would WE be? You see, the gift isn't just for you. It is also to help someone else. The business isn't just about you. It's about those who need your services and products. Going for that degree isn't just for you. It's about being an example for those who never felt higher education was possible. Trailblazers and pioneers do not become who they are with only themselves in mind. They make way for those coming behind them.

This book is bigger than me and once I realized that, I began writing. Once I realized that there are thousands, even millions of people who are afraid or doubtful about taking action, I knew there was a great need for this book. I took the attention off Alex and placed it on you. I placed my attention on the people I love, who have been stagnant for years. I placed my attention on my children. I placed my attention on a generation.

Esther was able to save her people by making a selfless, yet risky decision. Although going to the king was against the law, the lives of her people were her ultimate focus. She used her influence and favor with the king to save her people from being killed. I love the story about Esther because in it she makes a powerful statement that changes the whole game. She summons her people to fast and then says, "*I will go to the king, even though it is against the law. And if I perish, I perish.*" (Esther 4:16) Like what? Sis was serious about the lives of her people. She took a leap for a purpose and because she did, her people were saved and she became one of the most renowned queens in history. She took the focus off herself and took a leap for others.

I challenge you to find your WHY, and write it down (write them down if you have more than one). Focus on your why and then, LEAP!

TRAILBLAZERS
AND PIONEERS
DO NOT BECOME
WHO THEY ARE
WITH ONLY
THEMSELVES
IN MIND. THEY
MAKE WAY FOR
THOSE COMING
BEHIND THEM.

AFFIRMATION

This leap that I'm
preparing to take,
is bigger than me.

SCRIPTURES

1. Esther 4:16
2. Proverbs 3:27-28
3. Acts 20:24
4. Philippians 2:4

REFLECTION

I will leap because _____

_____

_____

CHAPTER 8

Ready. Set. LEAP!

So now that you've discovered your why, it's time to get started, it's time to leap!

Now, because I do not know exactly what your leap is (a book, a business, etc.), I cannot tell you how to leap. We are all leaping toward different goals. However, I am sure we are all asking the same question: *how do I get started?*

When the Lord instructed that I would write a book, my first question was 'how?' I had never written a book before IN MY LIFE. I didn't know where to start or how to even begin! Then, the Holy Spirit literally said, *"if you would just start typing, I will tell you what to write."* Amazing, right? All I had to do was start typing and it literally just flowed out of me. Seriously. From the outline to every chapter, it flowed out of me like water. Every morning I wrote a chapter because I partnered with the Holy Spirit. My starting point may look different from yours, but one thing I will say is that the Holy Spirit will guide you through. It does not matter if you are the first in your family do it, the Bible tells us that the Holy Spirit will teach you ALL things (*John 14:26*). Not some things, but ALL things. I truly believe we are reluctant to take leaps because we lack examples and unfortunately, believe we are incapable of succeeding. Not true! The Holy Spirit is a teacher and an enabler. The Holy Spirit is your righthand man, one hundred grand. He will also connect you with the right people to help you.

THE <u>HOLY SPIRIT</u> IS
YOUR <u>RIGHTHAND</u> <u>MAN</u>,
ONE HUNDRED GRAND.

It is perfectly fine to seek guidance and wisdom from people who have succeeded in the area you want to leap into. This helps you avoid some mistakes and alleviate challenges. So yes, take the class. Go to the conference. Send the email. Shoot the DM. Research and study. Learn from the mistakes others are willing to share. Get as much wisdom and knowledge as you can and then, LEAP! Proverbs 15:22 in the amplified version says, "*without consultation and wise advice, plans are frustrated, but with many counselors they are established and succeed.*"

When I first began writing this book, I went to a writers' workshop that was hosted by a great author! She had written multiple books and helped others as well. So, I made it a priority to attend so that I could get the help and guidance that I needed. I attended and received so much information—even information that I didn't know was important. From that day forward, the host was an integral part of my journey. She texted me to make sure I was on track. She helped me in the editing process, and even helped me published. These were all things I was concerned about before I started writing and God provided.

God will align you with the right people, but you have to take the first step. Trust and believe that once you leap, everything will work out better than you have imagined.

AFFIRMATION

When I leap,
God will take care
of the rest.

SCRIPTURES

1. Proverbs 1:5
2. Proverbs 15:22
3. John 14:26

REFLECTION

_____ (date), is the day I decided to LEAP!

CHAPTER 9

You get what you focus on.

I cannot stress how important your FOCUS is when you leap. Maintaining a SHARP LEVEL of FOCUS is a major key. When you take your leap, anything and everything will try to work against you to distract and deter you from your goals, tasks, etc. You must have what I like to call, a "flint focus." If you research what a **flint** is, you will find that it is a rock that was used in the Stone Age to create sharp tools such as knife blades and axes. A flint is so sharp that it creates other sharp tools *without changing its form*. A flint rock was valuable and craftsmen would travel miles to get it because their livelihoods depended on having sharp tools. The word flint reminds me of the scripture in Isaiah 50:7 (NIV) where Isaiah says, "...therefore have I set my face like flint, and I know I will not be put to shame." Isaiah was so focused on the Lord and His word that no one or nothing could distract, deter, upset, or frustrate him. That's the type of focus you are going to need. You have to be so focused that not a hater, or even the devil with his bald-headed self, can get you off track.

To focus is to concentrate. It is to direct your attention and focus. Your leap needs your attention and focus. If you look at a ballerina or a dancer, you rarely see them looking backwards or sideways as they leap forward. Yes, there are different types of leaps—front leap, side leap, switch leap, etc. However, their focus remains in the direction they are going. When you're driving to your destination, do you drive looking backwards? I sure hope NOT. You drive looking forward, your eyes are FOCUSED on what's ahead. You have a place—a destination that you have to get to, and the only way to arrive safely is to focus on the road and focus on the directions from your navigation system. The same way you drive, is the same way you're going to have to leap. Looking straight ahead.

As I wrote this book, I had MANY distractions, truly silly in nature. These distractions were mainly linked to people, and there always seemed to be an issue. My laptop had to be restored and guess who forgot to save their manuscript? Me. So, about two or three chapters from this book had disappeared. I became so discouraged that I didn't write for almost a week. But then I remembered my why, and refused to let anything else distract me. You may not have the same scenarios, but you must commit to being so focused, you must be so determined to succeed and accomplish your goal, that nothing or no one can get in the way.

The only way you will be able to focus is if you keep your mind and your eyes fixed on Jesus (*Hebrews 12:2*).

Set your face like a FLINT and FOCUS!

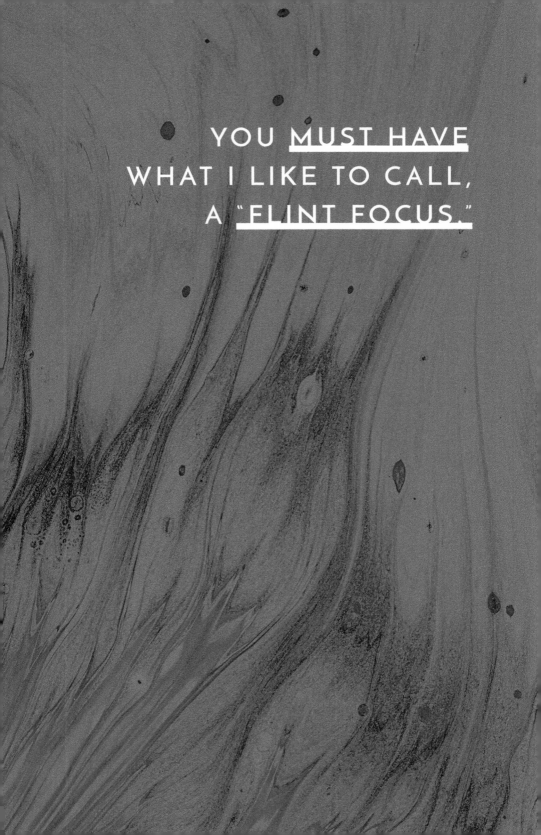

YOU <u>MUST HAVE</u>
WHAT I LIKE TO CALL,
A "<u>FLINT FOCUS.</u>"

AFFIRMATION

I will not be distracted. I will not be deterred. I will be FOCUSED.

SCRIPTURES

1. Isaiah 26:3
2. Isaiah 50:7
3. Proverbs 4:25
4. Hebrews 12:2

REFLECTION

I will maintain my focus by _____

_____

_____

CHAPTER 10

"Can't stop, won't stop."

DIDDY

Sometimes when I feel like giving up, I picture Diddy doing his infamous dance with his glasses tilted and halfway down his nose while saying, "can't stop, won't stop." Feel free to judge me, but that does two things for me:

1. It makes me laugh; and

2. It helps me to keep going.

I chose this topic for the last chapter of this book because I would be negligent if I failed to tell you an important truth. There will be times after you leap, when you feel like giving up. There may be times when you question if you really should have taken the leap. There may be late nights and early mornings, and there will be challenging times. You may shout, "I ain't never scared" in the beginning, but in the middle, you may start feeling that fear again. Who knows what your exact challenges will be, but know there will be some. Let this chapter, however, be your pick-me-up when you begin to feel like giving up. Let this chapter remind you that **you can't stop now, you can't give up now.** Let this chapter cause you to remember your why. Let this chapter cause you to overcome those battles with insecurities and put those doubts in their proper place. I want this chapter to remind you that God will give you the strength you need (Isaiah 40:29).

LEAP

Your leap has not, and will not go in vain. It wasn't a mistake; it wasn't a dumb decision. No matter how things look right now, you have to continue to walk by faith and not by sight (2 *Corinthians* 5:7). I reached a point in my journey where I almost gave up writing this book. I was exhausted. I began to feel insecure and to doubt myself again. I started to mentally tell myself that it's not going to be as great as I hoped it would be. I lost excitement, and I got discouraged. But then I began to think about all the people who needed this book. I began to think about how disappointed I would be in myself if I did not finish it. So, I kept going, tired and all. Now we're here and you're holding this book in your hand. You took a leap that you never thought you could or would.

You can and will do this. LEAP, and Diddy-shake your way to the finish line. You will be so proud of yourself, and others will thank you.

One final thing, don't forget to give God all the glory and honor. You could not have done it without Him.

AFFIRMATION

I will not give up.

I will not give in.

SCRIPTURES

1. Isaiah 40:29-31

2. Psalm 31:24

3. 2 Corinthians 12:9

4. 2 Corinthians 5:7

REFLECTION

Whenever I feel like giving up, I will _____

_____

_____ to keep myself going.

A CALL TO CHANGE

If you've read this book and not received Jesus as your Lord and Savior, I want to admonish you today, to do it. The greatest decision I have ever made, was surrendering my life to Jesus. Has it been easy? Nope. But it's been worth it and I would not trade this life to go back to my past. My past was very ugly, but ONE DECISION, changed my life for the better! The people connected to me have benefited from this change as well.

So today, I want to extend the invitation to salvation with Christ. All you have to do is say this prayer:

> Lord Jesus, for too long I've avoided you. For too long I've ran from you. I know that I am a sinner and that I cannot save myself. I need a Savior. No longer will I ignore your voice when I hear you speaking. No longer will I close the door when I hear you knocking. By faith I gratefully receive your gift of salvation. I am ready to trust you as my Lord and Savior. I am ready to experience your love. I am ready to be fathered by you. I am ready for change. Thank you, Lord Jesus, for coming to earth. I believe you are the Son of God who died on the cross for my sins and rose from the dead on the third day. Thank you for bearing my sins and giving me the gift of eternal life. I believe your words are true. Come into my heart, Lord Jesus, and be my Savior. Amen

"If you openly declare that Jesus is Lord and believe in your heart that God raised him from the dead, you will be saved. For it is by believing in your heart that you are made right with God, and it is by openly declaring your faith that you are saved."- Romans 10:9-10

ACKNOWLEDGEMENTS

To my Lord and Savior Jesus Christ, for being the first to LEAP. Thank you for being an eternal example and for entrusting me with a gift, a responsibility so GREAT. Thank you for literally breathing this book in and through me. You are the reason any of this is possible. All the Glory belongs to you.

To my fiancé, for believing in every idea that I have. Thank you for supporting everything I do, for looking at the multiple book covers I had before I chose a final one, for encouraging me in times of discouragement, for pushing me forward when I kept trying to push this project back, and for prophesying to my future. I love you.

To my family and friends, for your endless support. Thank you for being just as excited as I am. Thank you for cheering me on as I run this race. I am truly grateful.

To my leaders, Archbishop William Hudson III and Pastor Andria S. Hudson, for believing in this project and reading it, for agreeing to write the foreword and for your blessing to release it. Thank you.

To Latisha Morris, for inspiring me to write this book. Thank you for hosting an amazing and timely event for beginner authors like myself. Thank you for proofreading, for encouraging me in the process, and for making sure I had everything I needed. I appreciate you.

To Marlena Banks, author of *Big Idea Food*, thank you. Your work fueled me to finally take a leap and write this book. I am grateful for your advice in the process and that you shared your resources with me to make this happen.

To A'darah Adams, for bringing the vision of the book cover to life! Thank you for being patient with me and for allowing God to create through you.

To Denise Sarkor, for agreeing to accept this project. Thank you for taking the time to read, edit, and critique each page. Thank you for your input and suggestions that took this book to another level.

Finally, **to every person who reads this book**, thank you. You could have chosen any other book, but you picked this one. I pray it is a blessing to you.

ABOUT THE AUTHOR

Alexandria S. Norton is a rising millennial leader. A highly sought-after speaker, she has been established as one of today's voices for young women. The founder of IAMBELOVED—an organization geared toward enlightening, encouraging and empowering women to walk boldly in their purpose, she has focused her efforts on lifting others up. Professionally, she has interned for major enterprises as a project manager and today, she works as an associate brand manager for a multimillion dollar company, leveraging her Masters of Business Administration and Marketing concentration. As an active member of The Powerhouse Chicago, she also serves the community under the leadership of Archbishop William Hudson III and Pastor Andria Hudson. A mover and shaker, Alexandria travels far and wide to spread God's word while inspiring, encouraging and empowering a generation.

For more information, visit
www.leapthebook.org

CPSIA information can be obtained
at www.ICGtesting.com
Printed in the USA
FFHW020610091019
55426694-61184FF